Whales, Dolphins
and Sharks

Printed in the U.S.A. • ISBN: 1-40374-972-8
08 09 NGS 9 8 7 6 5 4 3 2

Gray Whale

The gray whale, like all whales, is a mammal that lives in the sea. And, like all mammals, it breathes air. The gray whale can hold its breath for 18 minutes under water, but it must come to the surface to take in air. Then it will "blow" excess water and carbon dioxide out of the blowhole in the top of its head. This forms a tall waterspout. The gray whale's spout can be 13 feet tall!

The gray whale really is gray and can be almost 50 feet long! Instead of a *dorsal* (back) fin, this whale has one fatty hump and some smaller bumps. Tiny critters, like barnacles, live on its skin.

The gray whale *migrates* (moves from place to place). It lives in the northern Pacific Ocean in the summer, and swims to warm lagoons (shallow waters) in Mexico in winter.

The gray whale is a "bottom feeder." It sucks up mud as far as 400 feet below the surface! With its tongue, it filters tiny *krill* (shrimp-like creatures) through the *baleen* (fringed plates) hanging from its upper jaw.

Baby Gray Whales

Gray whale calves are born in the winter in Mexico. Each female has one calf born almost 15 feet long!

What does it eat?
Krill, fish, and small squid.

Did You Know?

The gray whale does stunts, like jumping high out of the water, "riding" waves, rolling onto its side, and "waving" its fin.

Arctic Bowhead Whale

The bowhead whale has smooth, rubbery skin covered with an oily film to help it glide through the water. Beneath its skin is a thick layer of blubber, which protects it from the cold waters of the Arctic.

This whale can grow to be 60 feet long and weigh up to 90 tons. It has a great sense of hearing and, unlike some other whales, no bumps around its eyes, mouth, or blowhole.

The bowhead whale's mouth has hundreds of baleen plates that look like combs of thick hair. These hang from its upper jaw. When the whale closes its mouth, baleens strain the water, leaving krill and little fish behind.

What does it eat?
Krill, krill, krill—and little fish.

CREATURE FEATURE:
The bowhead whale is playful and curious!

3

Southern Right Whale

At about 60 feet long, this sea giant has a dark, rounded body, large flippers shaped like paddles, and bumps, called *callosities*, covering its huge head. Barnacles, worms, and whale lice live inside these hard callosities—coloring them white, yellow, pink, and orange.

Southern right whales live mostly in the open ocean.

CREATURE FEATURE:
The southern right whale sometimes performs "head standing"—swimming with its large tail out of the water. The whale uses its tail as a sail, letting the wind carry it along, like it's playing a game!

Did You Know?
Long ago, sailors thought these whales were the "right" ones to catch. Right whales live close to the coasts and have a lot of blubber. Since 1937, however, laws have saved many right whales from hunters.

4

Sei Whale

The sei whale is a kind of *rorqual* whale living in the waters from the Arctic to Antarctica. (Others are the fin whale and the blue whale, the largest animal in the world.)

The sei whale is gray, but *diatoms* (tiny algae) on its skin make it look blue.

Special grooves on this whale's throat help it gulp huge amounts of water. Then the sei whale uses its tongue to push the water out of its mouth; baleens hold back the krill.

Baby Sei Whales
In winter, sei whales migrate to warmer waters, and females give birth to calves in safe bays.

Humpback Whale

The gigantic humpback whale is about 50 feet long and weighs more than 20 tons! It has two long, white fins, and a tail that moves up and down.

The humpback whale has a huge head covered with wartlike bumps as big as golf balls! Each bump, or *tubercule*, has a hair in the center to sense things with.

This whale is slow but can leap almost all the way out of the water and fall back with a whopping splash! It comes up for air every three to ten minutes, but can stay under water for almost an hour.

Some humpbacks live only in northern waters; others only in the south.

CREATURE FEATURE: The humpback whale blows air out of its blowhole so hard that the spout can go 10 feet high.

What does it eat?
Krill and fish.

Baby Humpback Whales

In winter, southern humpback whales migrate north from their feeding grounds around Antarctica to Australia, southern Africa, and South America. In these warm waters—every three to four years—a female has a calf.

The two-ton calf swims close to its mother and, under water, is nursed on her milk. Every now and then, it comes up for air.

The Song

The humpback whale is famous for its long "song." A male uses his own special song to attract a mate. And if another male copies the melody, the whale just makes up a new tune!

Narwhal

Did You Know?

In the Middle Ages, people thought a narwhal's tusk was like a unicorn's. The tusk was also believed to have healing powers.

The narwhal is a mammal that grows to be about 14–16 feet long. It lives in the Arctic Sea on the edge of the pack ice, and in winter it follows the growth of the ice southward, returning north in the summer.

Narwhals live in separate pods (groups) that are either all males, or all females with calves. The color of this creature's skin changes with age: calves are grayish-brown; adults are mottled gray; and older narwhals are white.

CREATURE FEATURE:
Narwhals have only two teeth (canines) in their upper jaw, and in males, the left one grows into a tusk that can be 8 feet long and weigh 22 pounds! Scientists are not sure why narwhals have this tusk. Perhaps it's to show females who is the biggest and strongest.

Beluga Whale

This sea creature is about the same size as the narwhal. It has a rounded forehead, no *dorsal* (back) fin, and a thick layer of blubber to keep it warm in the cold Arctic Sea. A beluga's skin is white, making it hard to spot around blocks of ice. It likes to be with other animals, swimming slowly and gracefully in pods, and "talking" with chirps, whistles, squawks, and clicks. It eats fish, squid, and crustaceans.

Baby Beluga Whales

Beluga calves weigh 175 pounds at birth and are nursed by their mothers for about a year. Their skin is slate gray but lightens as they grow up, until becoming white.

Orca

The orca is the largest member of the dolphin family. At birth, this sea creature is already more than 6½ feet long!

When it grows up, the male can be about 30 feet long. Its triangle-shaped dorsal fin alone can be more than 6 feet tall!

Orcas have dark skin with white areas. They are very smart and usually live in pods with six to thirty members. The pods have male and female orcas of all ages—mostly family members who stay together their whole lives. Members "talk" with whistles, squeals, and clicks.

These dolphins live in all the oceans, but they like the cold polar regions most.

Did You Know?

Sometimes an orca uses its nose to break thick sheets of ice where seals are resting. Then the seals fall into the ocean!

Baby Orcas

Between November and December, the female gives birth to a calf that is about 6 feet long and 400 pounds. She nurses her calf for more than a year.

What does it eat?

Dolphins, seals, sharks, sea tortoises, fish, seabirds, walruses, and even blue whales. Orcas use a special *sonar* (sound) system to locate their prey. Each orca has 10-13 pairs of long, sharp teeth. It hunts alone or in pods.

CREATURE FEATURE:
Orcas are amazing acrobats. They are often the stars at theme parks!

Risso's Dolphin

The Risso's dolphin can be 11 feet long. Its skin becomes covered with white scars—battle scars from fights with its "cousins," and squid, a favorite prey.

Risso's dolphins like to swim in deep, warm waters and hunt in groups, side by side.

Baby Risso's Dolphins

This baby dolphin is gray at birth and gets lighter as it grows up, becoming almost white when it's old.

Striped Dolphin

The striped dolphin is small, with a sleek body about 8 feet long. This dolphin has clear lines on its sides, with a dark back, gray flanks, a white or rosy-colored belly, and dark patches around the eyes.

Striped dolphins eat fish, mollusks, and crustaceans. They can dive 650 feet in search of food and stay under water for ten minutes!

CREATURE FEATURE:
Striped dolphins are good acrobats. They can jump up to 23 feet above the water, perform backward summersaults, and do amazing flips!

Common Dolphin

The common dolphin is about 8 feet long and 220 pounds—but it swims quickly.

The dolphin surfaces regularly to breathe, using a blowhole on its head. And in its mouth are 40 to 50 tiny sharp teeth.

These dolphins like warm, open ocean waters, but sometimes they will explore gulfs and bays, and even swim far upstream in rivers. They live together in herds that can number in the thousands. They "talk" to each other with whistles, squeals, and clicks.

Baby Common Dolphins

In spring, the female gives birth to one calf. Newborns nurse for a year but stay with the mother until they are two. The herd protects the young from predators, and when a calf is tired, the mother lifts it onto her back and swims along the surface.

Did You Know?

Dolphins sleep while swimming slowly on the surface of the waves. They keep their heads out of the water to breathe. Their tails move "by reflex," even when they're asleep!

13

Dolphin

Dolphins are lively animals. They love to leap out of the water, somersaulting, and swimming backward while holding themselves upright. They also like to ride the waves in front of ships' bows.

To hunt, the dolphin uses sonar. It sends out *ultrasounds* (sound waves) that hit obstacles, like schools of fish or a fishing boat. These sound waves bounce off the objects and the echo returns to the dolphin. Then a special organ in the dolphin's head tells it what objects are nearby and how close they are.

By day, dolphins move in herds, hunting schools of fish, like sardines, in the open sea. At night, dolphins hunt in the deep ocean, going down as far as 920 feet. They can hold their breath for at least five minutes to catch fish, mollusks, and *cephalopods*, like squid.

Did You Know?

Dolphins are smart and curious. Sometimes they swim up to scuba divers and travel alongside them.

Blind River Dolphin

The blind river dolphin is a freshwater dolphin that is almost extinct. It is now rarely found in some of the biggest rivers of northern India. Its eyes are tiny and almost useless, but these dolphins use their own echo system to find their way around in the murky waters.

Did You Know?

Much calmer and quieter than its sea-living cousins, this dolphin lives in small groups of three to ten. Little families of blind river dolphins usually swim downstream in rivers in the winter and back upstream during the summer rainy season.

Amazon River Dolphin

The Amazon River dolphin lives only in fresh water, in the Amazon, Orinoco, and Rio Negro basins of South America. It has a long *rostrum* (snout) and a high forehead.

This dolphin's skin color can be dark gray to light gray or even pink! It lives alone or in groups of about twelve, and comes up often for air.

Did You Know?

These mammals have such a good sonar system that it's very hard to catch them with nets. The dolphin senses the trap and jumps over it.

What does it eat?

Mainly fish—even ferocious piranhas!

Whitetip Reef Shark

Unlike whales and dolphins, sharks are fish, not mammals. The whitetip reef shark has a gray-and-white body that can grow to be 6½ feet long. A little white mark on the tip of its dorsal fin gives this shark its name.

The whitetip reef shark lives with its "cousins" within a few square miles in shallow waters or lagoons. It swims lazily and can dive 130 feet. This shark rests during the day and hunts at night.

Baby Whitetip Reef Sharks

Females give birth when they are about five years old. They have one to five little sharks at a time. At birth, the newborns are 3½ feet long and can already take care of themselves.

CREATURE FEATURE:
Sharks have no bones—only cartilage (firm tissue).

Great White Shark

This light-colored shark has a stocky body and can grow to be more than 30 feet long!

The great white has a reputation for attacking lifeguards and surfers, but it really likes to stay away from the coast in deep waters. Since this shark does not see well, it can mistake people for its usual prey.

CREATURE FEATURE:
The great white's tail works like a propeller to help it swim very fast.

What does it eat?
Fish, seals, and marine turtles. The great white's mouth has rows of triangle-shaped, razor-sharp teeth about 3 inches long.

Tiger Shark

The tiger shark has a huge body, about 26 feet long. Young sharks look striped but become gray on top and off-white underneath as they age. (These stripes give the shark its name.)

Tiger sharks swim alone in tropical and subtropical seas. They also circle around ports and coral reefs, and they like cloudy water.

Baby Tiger Sharks

The female tiger shark has pups that are 2 feet long and can already take care of themselves.

What does it eat?
Because of its strong, serrated (notched) teeth, the tiger shark can catch many animals—fish, birds, turtles, and other sharks.

Blue Shark

This shark, also called a blue dog or a blue pointer, is usually a deep indigo blue color on top and white underneath. It can be almost 13 feet long. Newborn pups are only about 16 inches.

The blue shark, which has long, pointed fins, is one of the world's fastest sharks. Some scientists believe it can swim up to 60 mph!

This shark groups in all-male or all-female schools that travel near the surface of the ocean, except in tropical waters, where it goes deeper.

What does it eat?
Slippery squid and fish, like herring or cod, and sometimes seals.

Small Spotted Cat Shark

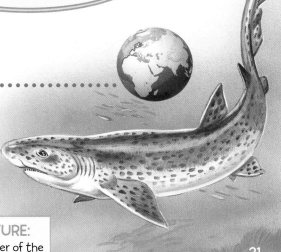

This slender gray-brown shark has a light belly and spots on its sides and fins. It is a bottom-dweller that feeds on small fish, mollusks, and crustaceans. The cat shark can grow to be about 3½ feet long. It lives in the eastern and northern Atlantic Ocean and the Mediterranean Sea. It is harmless to humans.

CREATURE FEATURE:
The best-known member of the cat shark family is the dogfish!

21

Hammerhead Shark

The hammerhead shark is 13 feet long and has a head that really looks like a hammer! The head has big *frontal lobes* about 3 feet long. At the end of each lobe are an eye and a nostril. This shape helps the shark see and smell and move through the water well.

The hammerhead shark, a fast swimmer, tends to stay away from things that bother it—like divers.

CREATURE FEATURE:
Sometimes, hammerhead sharks get together in groups of up to 100!

Stingray

Stingrays are related to sharks. Like sharks, they have only cartilage and no bones. They are broad, flat fish with wide *pectoral* (side) fins that they flap to move through the water. Stingrays can grow up to 10 feet long.

The stingray gets its name from its barbed tail, which can deliver a poisonous—and deadly—sting!

What does it eat?
Mollusks and crustaceans sucked up from the sand.

Manta Ray

This big, flat fish gets its name from the Spanish word *manta*, meaning coat or blanket. A manta ray weighs up to 3,000 pounds, and when its fins are spread out, it can be 30 feet wide!

This ray is blue-black on its back and white underneath. It eats *microorganisms* (tiny creatures too small to be seen) by filtering them down its throat.

Some mantas live alone. Others join groups as big as 50. But whether alone or in a group, the manta ray can migrate hundreds of miles.

Baby Manta Rays

A newborn manta ray is about 5 feet wide and has fins that are folded—one along the back and the other along the abdomen. After birth, the little ray's fins spread out like a butterfly.

CREATURE FEATURE:
The manta ray usually glides slowly along, but it can also jump out of the water!

Did You Know?
Sailors called the manta "devil of the seas" because its winglike fins looked like big horns.

23

Whale Shark

Though it is not a whale, at 25–46 feet long, the whale shark is the biggest fish in the world. Its huge body is lined with white markings and stripes, and its mouth can be 4 feet wide! In some places, the whale shark's skin is 4 inches thick.

The whale shark migrates in open seas, but also likes to hang around coral reefs to feed on little fish and *plankton* (tiny organisms). The whale shark has about 3,000 little teeth, but it is a filter feeder, so it is no danger to humans.

CREATURE FEATURE:
Whale sharks may live 100–150 years!